Zen Cats

MEDITATIONS FOR THE WISE MINDS OF CAT LOVERS

Buddha
and the editors of
Mango Media

Cover Design: Roberto Nuñez
Interior Layout: Roberto Nuñez
Front Cover Images:
- Ermolaev Alexander/Shutterstock
- fotohunter/Shutterstock

Maria A. Llorens/Mango Media, Inc.
100 Miracle Mile, Suite 200
Miami, FL 33134
www.mangomedia.us

Publisher's Note: This is a work of nonfiction. Names, characters, places, and incidents are based on historical fact. Locales and public names are sometimes used for informative purposes. Any resemblance to actual people, living or dead, or to businesses, companies, events, institutions, or locales is completely coincidental.

Zen Cats: Meditations for the Wise Minds of Cat Lovers
Maria A. Llorens/Mango Media Inc. -- 1st ed.
ISBN 978-1-63353-048-5

"Whether one believes in a religion or not, and whether one believes in rebirth or not, there isn't anyone who doesn't appreciate kindness and compassion."

Tenzin Gyatso, the 14th Dalai Lama

TABLE OF CONTENTS

VIRTUE   68

TRUTH   **108**

MIND
AND
BODY

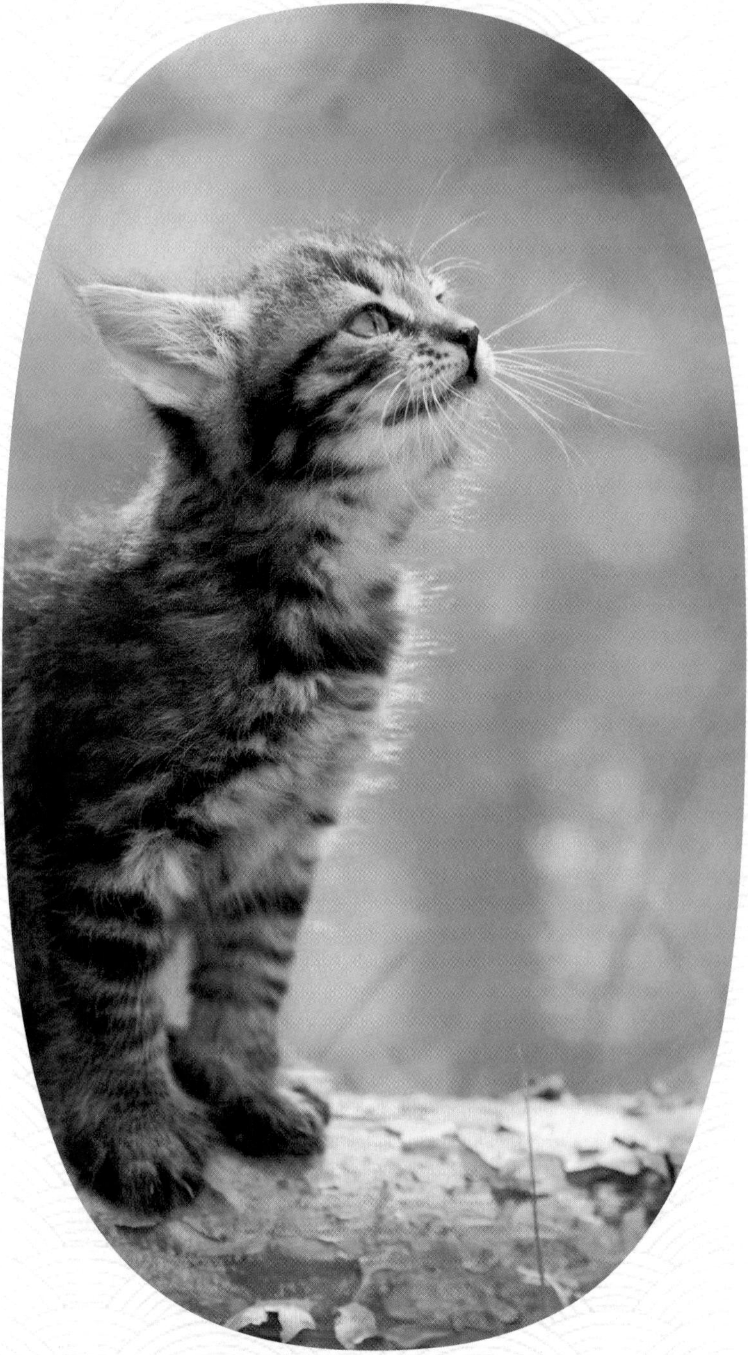

VERSE 1

All that we are is the result
of what we have thought: it
is founded on our thoughts,
it is made up of our thoughts.
If a man speaks or acts with
a pure thought, happiness
follows him, like a shadow
that never leaves him.

You are what you think. If you're dwelling on negative
thoughts—jealousy, anger, resentment—they will become
part of your character. Focus that energy on thoughts that
make you a better and smarter person.

VERSE 2

For hatred does not cease by hatred
at any time: hatred ceases by love,
this is an old rule.

Focus on loving something rather than the thing you hate.

VERSE 3

He who lives without looking for pleasures, his senses well controlled, moderate in his food, faithful and strong, him evil will certainly not overthrow, any more than the wind throws down a rocky mountain.

Relying on creature comforts will skew your perspective. Let them enhance your mood, not control it.

VERSE 4

As rain breaks through an ill-thatched house, passion will break through an unreflecting mind.

Guard your mind from bouts of anger or irritability with thoughts and activities that make you happy.

VERSE 5

It is good to tame the mind, which is difficult to hold in and flighty, rushing wherever it listeth; a tamed mind brings happiness.

Your mind can easily be taken over by hectic days and stress. Set aside quiet time to regroup and reflect.

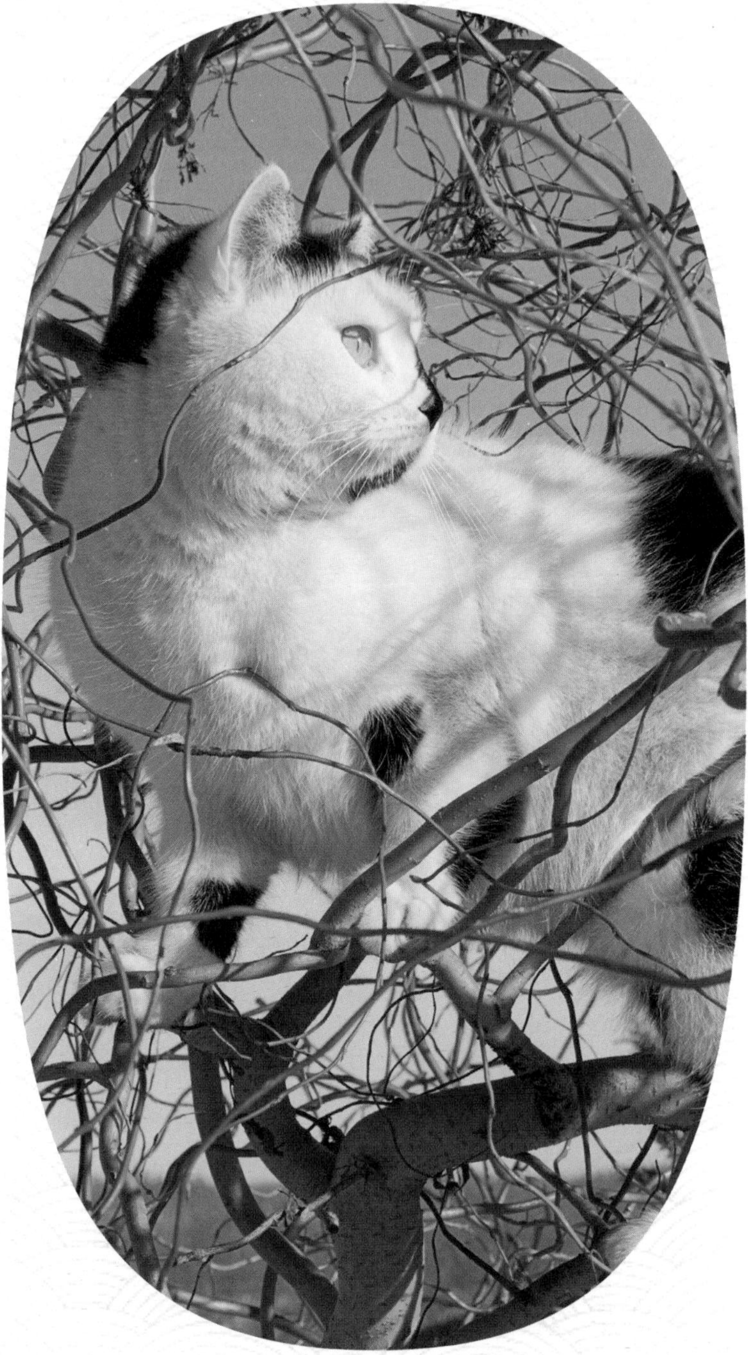

VERSE 6

If a man's thoughts are unsteady, if he does not know the true law, if his peace of mind is troubled, his knowledge will never be perfect.

Make time to reflect on the good and bad in your life. A reflective mind allows knowledge to build within it.

VERSE 7

Knowing that this body is fragile like a jar, and making this thought firm like a fortress, one should attack Mara (the tempter) with the weapon of knowledge, one should watch him when conquered, and should never rest.

Empathy comes from knowledge. You'll get better at avoiding what's bad for you if you know how to recognize it. Think of how your actions affect you and others.

VERSE 8

Long is the night to him who is awake; long is a mile to him who is tired; long is life to the foolish who do not know the true law.

Life will seem like an endless slog unless you enrich your life with actions that help you and others.

VERSE 9

Those whose mind is well grounded in the elements of knowledge, who without clinging to anything, rejoice in freedom from attachment, whose appetites have been conquered, and who are full of light, are free even in this world.

The knowledge that your desires are fleeting will allow you freedom to make more fulfilling choices, rather than being a slave to the material.

VERSE 10

His thought is quiet, quiet are his word and deed, when he has obtained freedom by true knowledge, when he has thus become a quiet man.

The world is filled with endless chatter. Use your words to enrich others. Make them think or simply laugh.

VERSE 11

If one man conquer in battle a thousand times thousand men, and if another conquer himself, he is the greatest of conquerors.

Battling your weaknesses will always be a more worthy battle than trying to fight others.

VERSE 12

Do not speak harshly to anybody; those who are spoken to will answer thee in the same way. Angry speech is painful, blows for blows will touch thee.

Disagreements are part of life. Kind words will lead to enlightenment, harsh ones to fighting.

VERSE 13

By oneself the evil is done, by oneself one suffers; by oneself evil is left undone, by oneself one is purified. Purity and impurity belong to oneself, no one can purify another.

No one has the power to change your character. Use that advantage to become the best version of yourself as you see fit.

VERSE 14

Even in heavenly pleasures he finds
no satisfaction, the disciple who is
fully awakened delights only in the
destruction of all desires.

Hunger, lust, envy—these things are temporary.
Hunger instead for creating good things for
yourself and others.

VERSE 15

Hunger is the worst of diseases, the body the greatest of pains; if one knows this truly, that is Nirvana, the highest happiness.

Happiness will not come from filling material desires, but from rejecting them for greater goals.

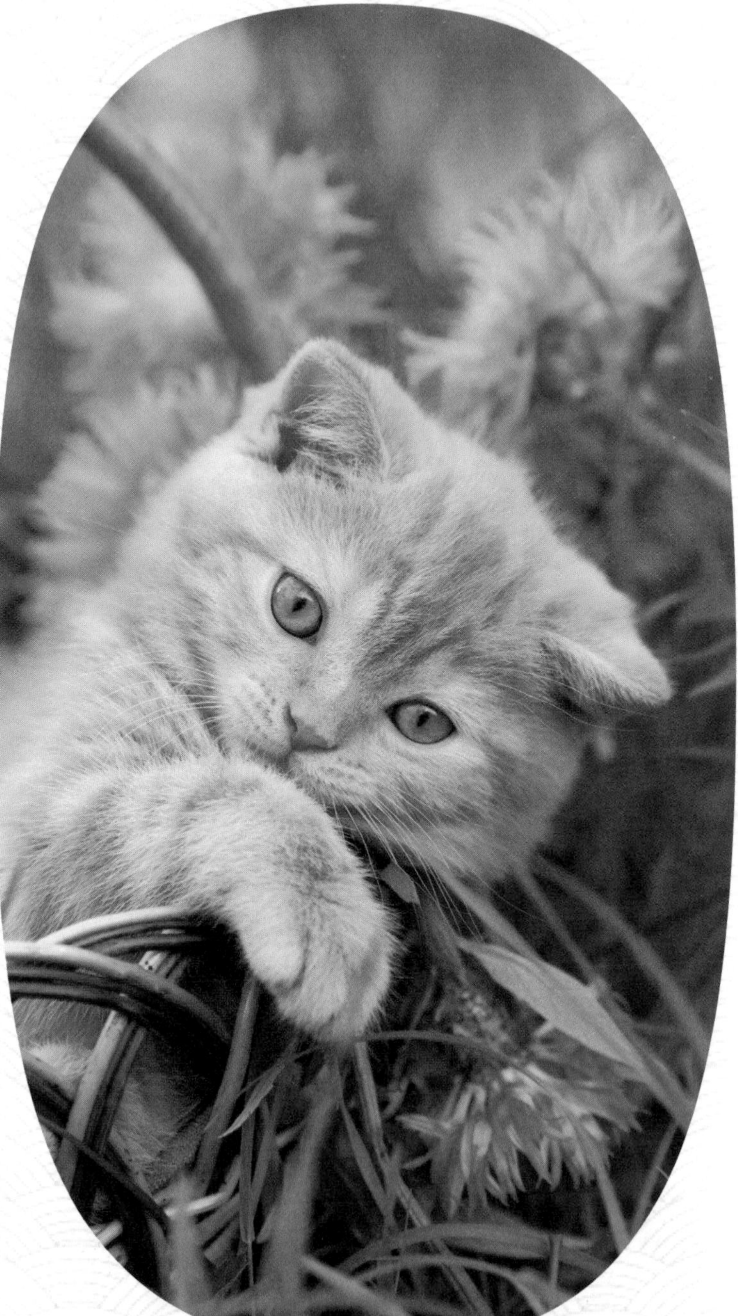

VERSE 16

From lust comes grief, from lust comes fear; he who is free from lust knows neither grief nor fear.

Excessive lust can complicate your life, bringing fear, sadness, and jealousy to others. Honesty in relationships will benefit all areas of your life.

VERSE 17

Make thyself an island, work hard, be wise!
When thy impurities are blown away, and
thou art free from guilt, thou wilt not enter
again into birth and decay.

Focusing on hard work and wise thoughts will simplify
your life. You'll be happier without the noise.

VERSE 18

If a man looks after the faults of others,
and is always inclined to be offended,
his own passions will grow, and he is far
from the destruction of passions.

It's better to help friends than criticize them.
Offer kind advice when needed.

VERSE 19

He who does not rouse himself when it is time to rise, who, though young and strong, is full of sloth, whose will and thought are weak, that lazy and idle man will never find the way to knowledge.

A healthy body and mind is a gift, use it to live up to your potential.

VERSE 20

This mind of mine went formerly wandering about as it liked, as it listed, as it pleased; but I shall now hold it in thoroughly, as the rider who holds the hook in the furious elephant.

Calm your mind when it feels like it's in a million places. Focus only on what is most important.

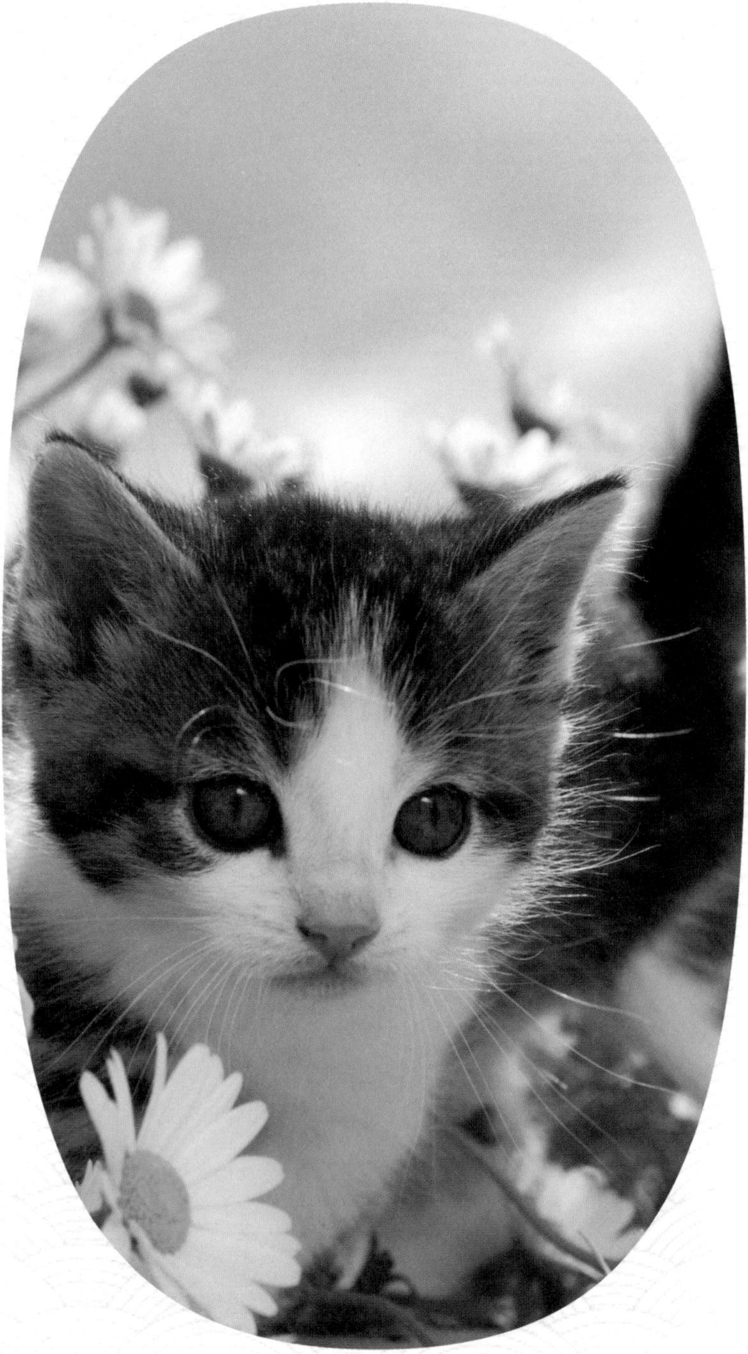

VERSE 21

He who overcomes this fierce thirst, difficult to be conquered in this world, sufferings fall off from him, like water-drops from a lotus leaf.

When you send your material needs away, your unhappiness will leave with them.

VERSE 22

Men, driven on by thirst, run about like a snared hare; held in fetters and bonds, they undergo pain for a long time, again and again.

Bodily and material desires will drive you crazy if you let them. You'll become a more complete, spiritual person without them.

VERSE 23

If a man is tossed about by doubts, full of strong passions, and yearning only for what is delightful, his thirst will grow more and more, and he will indeed make his fetters strong.

Practice makes perfect, and that applies to good habits too. You have truly become better when doing the right thing feels natural.

VERSE 24

The fields are damaged by weeds, mankind is damaged by vanity: therefore a gift bestowed on those who are free from vanity brings great reward.

Vanity, like a weed, takes over your self-perception. Relying on others for affirmation distorts your sense of right and wrong and of your worth.

VERSE 25

Restraint in the eye is good, good is restraint in the ear, in the nose restraint is good, good is restraint in the tongue.

Many ideas, thoughts and people will come along your path. Determine which ones are worth listening to.

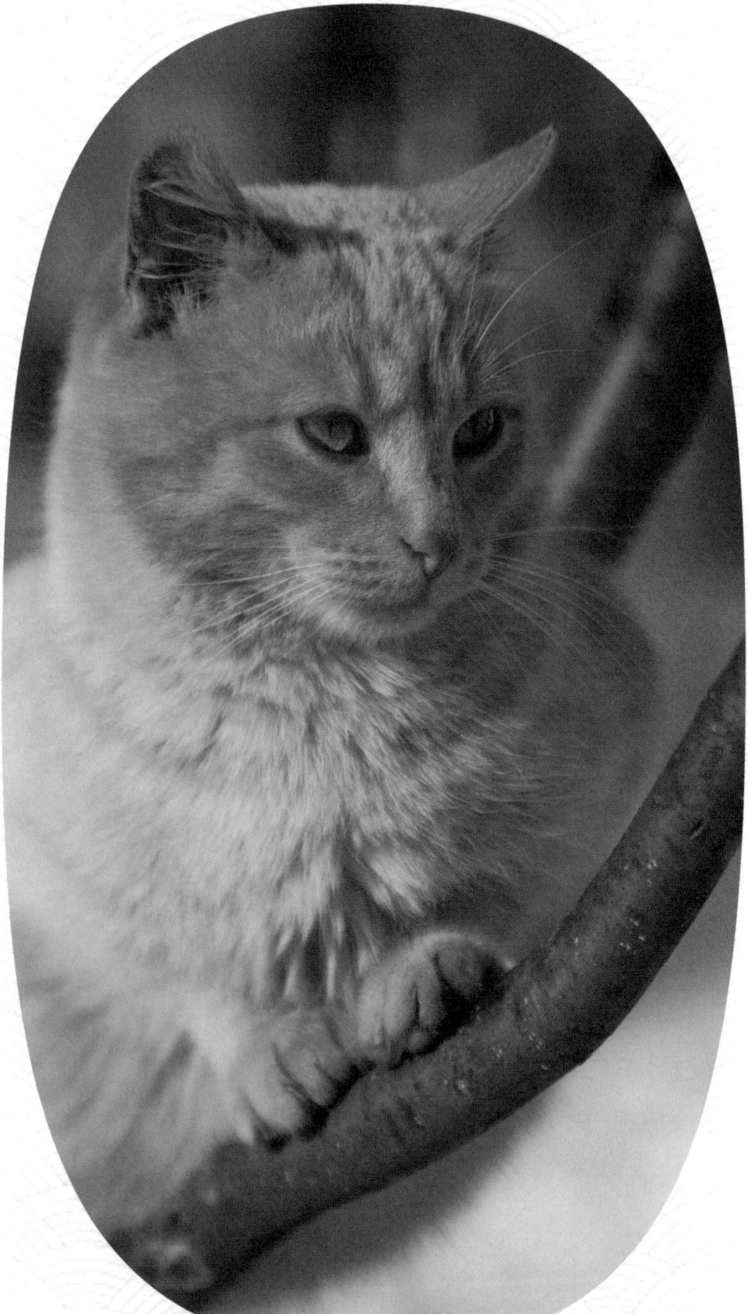

VERSE 26

For self is the lord of self, self is the refuge of self; therefore curb thyself as the merchant curbs a good horse.

You're the master of your mind, and only you can control how it works. Train yourself to be better. No one else can.

VERSE 27

Stop the stream valiantly, drive away
the desires, O Brahmana! When you
have understood the destruction of all
that was made, you will understand
that which was not made.

Petty desires can become like a flooded river, destroying
so many possibilities of growth and happiness. Always rise
above them with thoughtfulness and knowledge.

VERSE 28

Him I call enlightened who does not offend by body, word, or thought, and is controlled on these three points.

Enlightenment doesn't come from accolades or material possessions. It comes simply from achieving balance in your body and curiosity for wise thoughts.

VERSE 29

I do not call a man
enlightened because of his
origin or of his mother. He
is indeed arrogant, and he is
wealthy: but the poor, who
is free from all attachments,
him I call indeed enlightened.

People who rely on social or financial status to feel
important will inevitably lose sight of what matters.
Keep those things secondary to your true purpose.

HAPPINESS

VERSE 30

"He abused me, he beat me, he defeated me, he robbed me," —in those who harbour such thoughts hatred will never cease.

There are better uses of your time than holding grudges. Accept what you can't change, and accept apologies when they're offered.

VERSE 31

Follow not after vanity, nor after the enjoyment of love and lust! He who is earnest and meditative, obtains ample joy.

You'll find more long-term joy from earnestness and solitude than from short-term pleasures, like vanity.

VERSE 32

Let the wise man guard his thoughts, for they are difficult to perceive, very artful, and they rush wherever they list: thoughts well guarded bring happiness.

It's better to let your thoughts brew a bit than reveal them to others before they're ready. It's as simple as "think before you speak."

VERSE 33

"These sons belong to me, and this wealth belongs to me," with such thoughts a fool is tormented. He himself does not belong to himself; how much less sons and wealth?

Your success is a gift. Share it with others and it will bring you more happiness than from its mere existence.

52

VERSE 34

Good people walk on whatever befall, the good do not prattle, longing for pleasure; whether touched by happiness or sorrow wise people never appear elated or depressed.

Ride the wave, whether it's smooth or choppy. The bad times won't knock you off your feet, and the good times won't blind you to reality.

VERSE 35

He who always greets and constantly reveres the aged, four things will increase to him—life, beauty, happiness, power.

Appreciate your elders, and you'll reap the rewards of their influence and wisdom.

VERSE 36

If a man does what is good, let him do it again; let him delight in it: happiness is the outcome of good.

If you do something good, repeat it. Hold on to the feeling it creates and use it to ward off temptation.

VERSE 37

Even a good man sees evil days, as long as
his good deed has not ripened; but when
his good deed has ripened, then does
the good man see happy days.

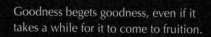

Goodness begets goodness, even if it
takes a while for it to come to fruition.

VERSE 38

He who seeking his own happiness punishes
or kills beings who also long for happiness,
will not find happiness after death.

People who you think are your enemies want the
same things you do: happiness and success.

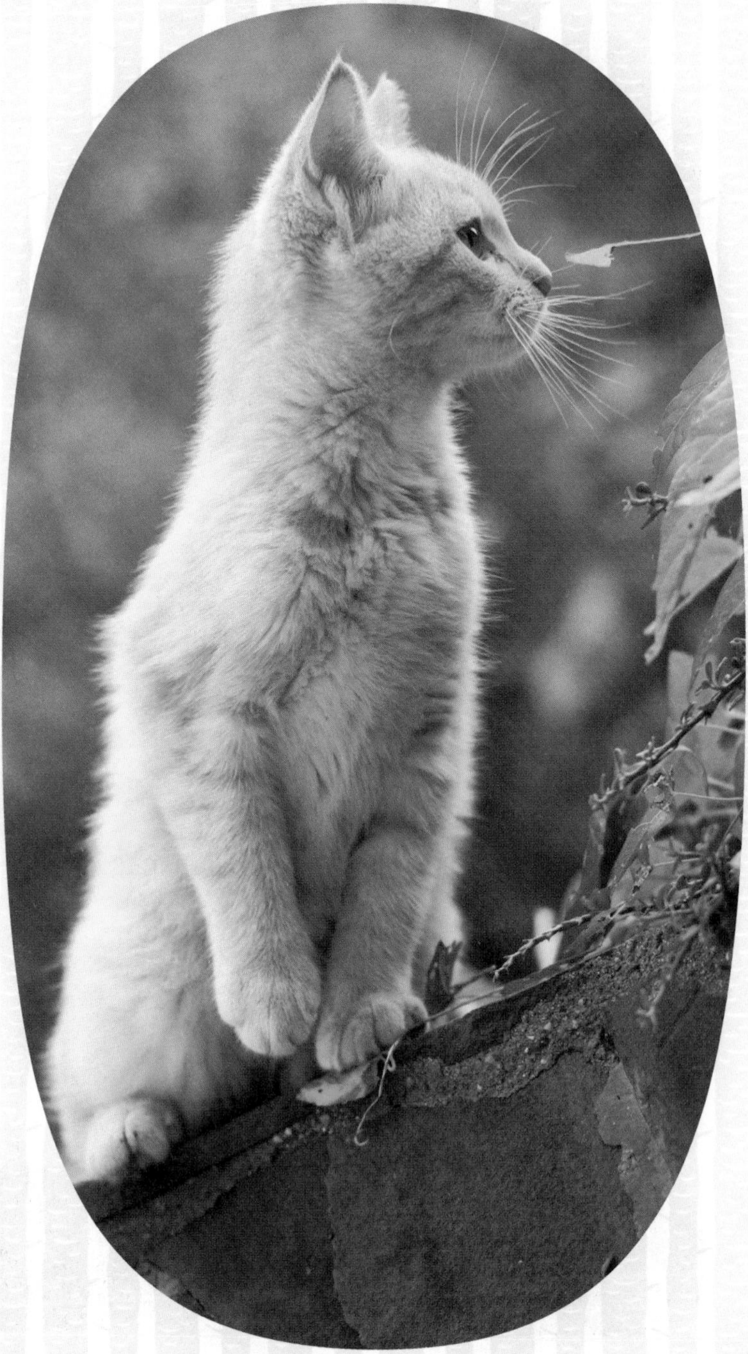

VERSE 39

Victory breeds hatred, for the conquered is unhappy. He who has given up both victory and defeat, he, the contented, is happy.

You're better off working with others than competing, whether at work or in your personal life.

VERSE 40

Health is the greatest of gifts,
contentedness the best riches; trust
is the best of relationships, Nirvana
the highest happiness.

Appreciate your health, trust your loved ones, and be thankful
for what you have. You'll be closer to heaven that way.

VERSE 41

He who, by causing pain to others,
wishes to obtain pleasure for himself,
he, entangled in the bonds of hatred,
will never be free from hatred.

Happiness will come undone if it is based on others' pain.

VERSE 42

An act carelessly performed, a broken vow,
and hesitating obedience to discipline, all
this brings no great reward.

Discipline in work strengthens the mind to
avoid carelessness in all things.

VERSE 43

The fields are damaged by weeds, mankind is damaged by hatred: therefore a gift bestowed on those who do not hate brings great reward.

Strive to be kind, even with strangers.

VERSE 44

Him I call indeed enlightened from whom anger and hatred, pride and envy have dropt like a mustard seed from the point of a needle.

Enlightenment comes from abandoning the distracting emotions that come from selfishness.

VERSE 45

Him I call indeed enlightened who is bright like the moon, pure, serene, undisturbed, and in whom all gaiety is extinct.

Living serenely, unbothered by daily tribulations, will lead to a more purposeful life.

VERSE 46

Him I call indeed enlightened who, leaving all longings, travels about without a home, and in whom all covetousness is extinct.

The less attachment you have to the material, the more room you have to enjoy the spiritual joys of life.

VIRTUE

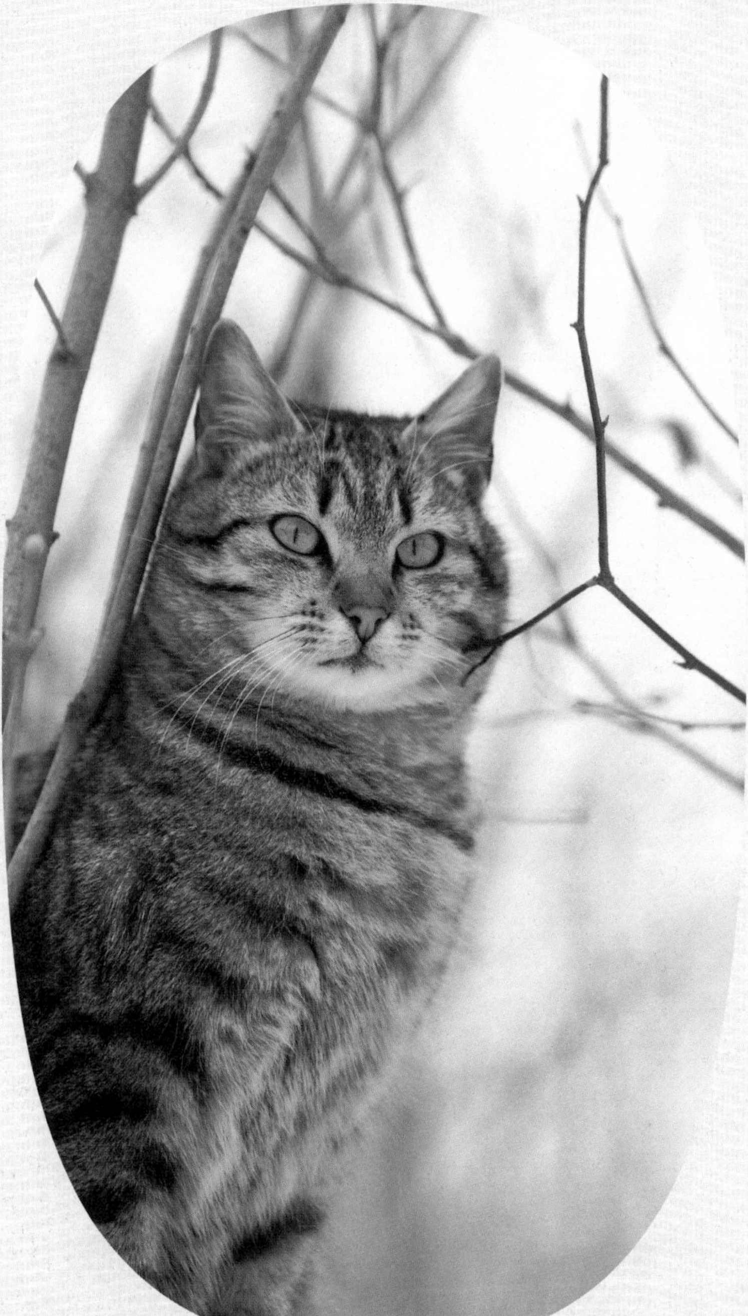

VERSE 47

These wise people,
meditative, steady, always
possessed of strong powers,
attain to Nirvana, the
highest happiness.

While many desirable things, like money, can't promise
happiness, pursuing wisdom and self-control can.

VERSE 48

By rousing himself, by earnestness, by restraint and control, the wise man may make for himself an island which no flood can overwhelm.

Restraint and earnestness are your guides to navigating the storms of life.

VERSE 49

Fools follow after vanity, men of evil wisdom. The wise man keeps earnestness as his best jewel.

An honest character is worth much more than any sum of money and will bring more happiness. Appearances can fool you.

VERSE 50

Earnest among the thoughtless, awake among the sleepers, the wise man advances like a racer, leaving behind the hack.

Though it may seem unjust that immoral people are getting ahead in life, it's the wise man that wins in the end.

VERSE 51

As the bee collects nectar and departs without injuring the flower, or its colour or scent, so let a sage dwell in his village.

Leave the world a little better than you found it.
A single good person makes a difference.

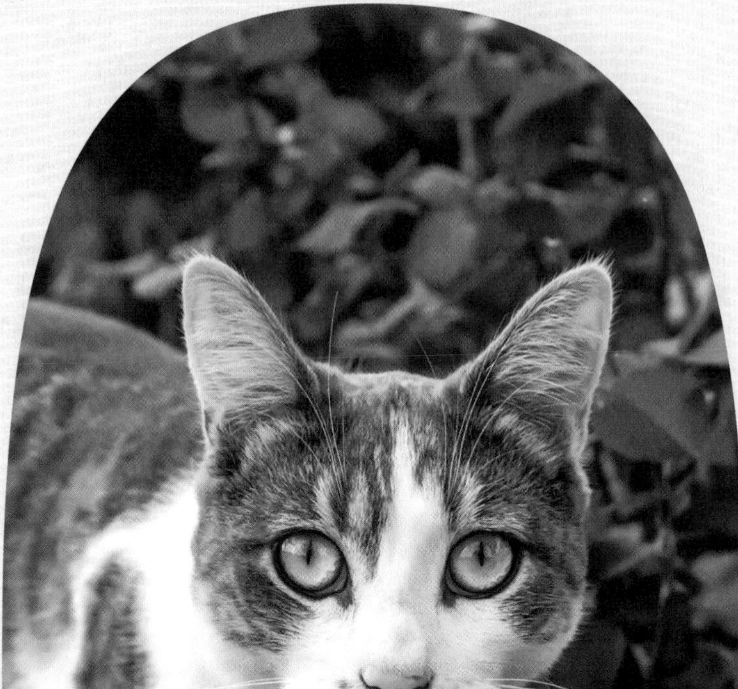

VERSE 52

Not the perversities of others,
not their sins of commission
or omission, but his own
misdeeds and negligences
should a sage take notice of.

Everyone has enough on their own plate. There is no
need to focus on others' imperfections.

VERSE 53

Like a beautiful flower, full of colour and full of scent, are the fine and fruitful words of him who acts accordingly.

Make it so your actions and words add beauty to others' lives.

VERSE 54

As many kinds of wreaths can be made from a heap of flowers, so many good things may be achieved by a mortal when once he is born.

Your life has endless potential. Create many things and be giving with yourself. You'll feel like your time was well-spent.

VERSE 55

Mean is the scent that comes from
Tagara and sandalwood;—the perfume
of those who possess virtue rises up
to the gods as the highest.

Spiritual gifts will always enrich your life more
than the material. Those who say otherwise
have not achieved wisdom.

VERSE 56

Fools of little understanding have themselves for their greatest enemies, for they do evil deeds which must bear bitter fruits.

Everything you choose to do will have an effect on your well-being, so be wise with your choices.

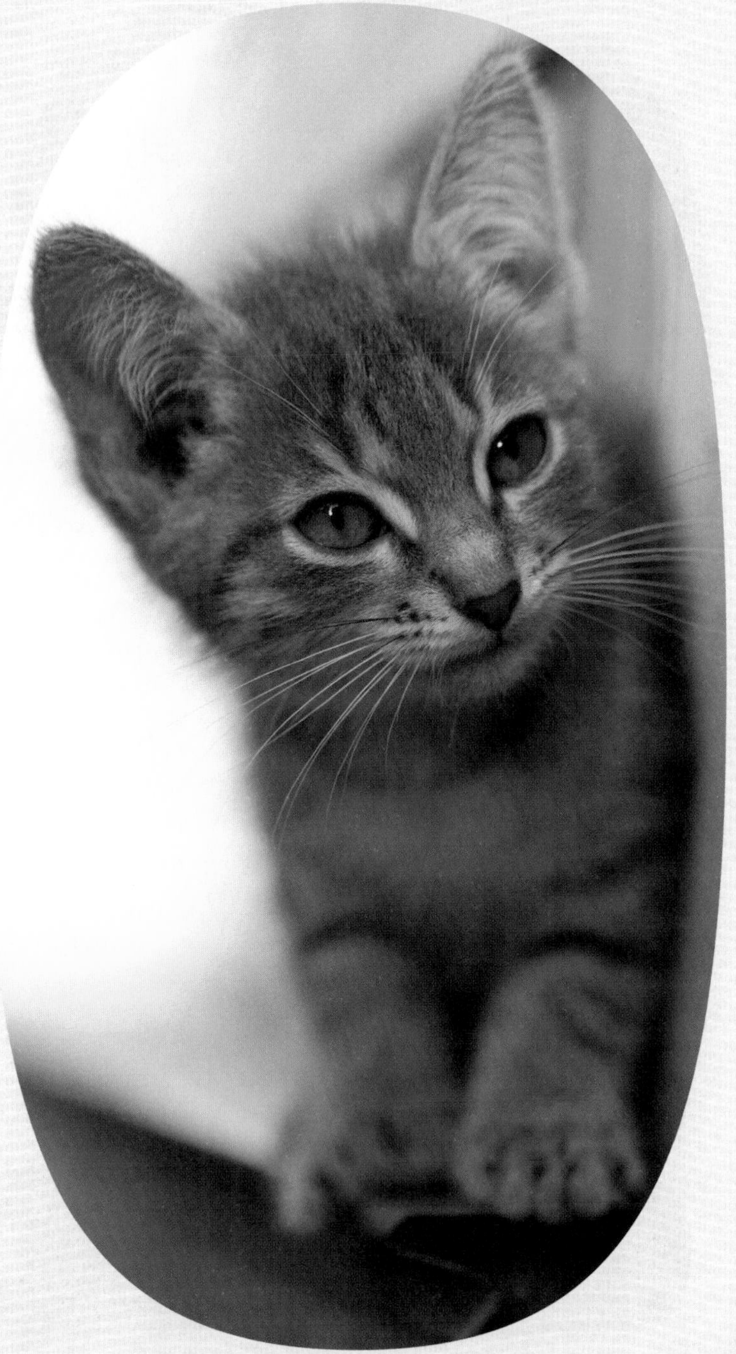

VERSE 57

As long as the evil deed done does not bear fruit, the fool thinks it is like honey; but when it ripens, then the fool suffers grief.

Even if you aren't caught for an evil deed, it will come back to hurt you later.

VERSE 58

Let him admonish, let him teach, let him forbid
what is improper!—he will be beloved of the
good, by the bad he will be hated.

Many people are threatened by good ideas, because they see
it as a judgment on their actions. Speak your mind anyway.

VERSE 59

Do not have evil-doers for friends, do not have
low people for friends: have virtuous people
for friends, have for friends the best of men.

Your friends can't change you, but they can
influence your choices.

VERSE 60

If, whether for his own sake, or for the sake of others, a man wishes neither for a son, nor for wealth, nor for lordship, and if he does not wish for his own success by unfair means, then he is good, wise, and virtuous.

Work to obtain a good mind and a good heart to get you through the inevitable ups-and-downs of life.

VERSE 61

He whose appetites are stilled, who is not absorbed in enjoyment, who has perceived void and unconditioned freedom (Nirvana), his path is difficult to understand, like that of birds in the air.

It's difficult to perceive of a life free from indulgence and desire—we're human, after all. But it's more rewarding and exhilarating to free yourself from those dull constraints.

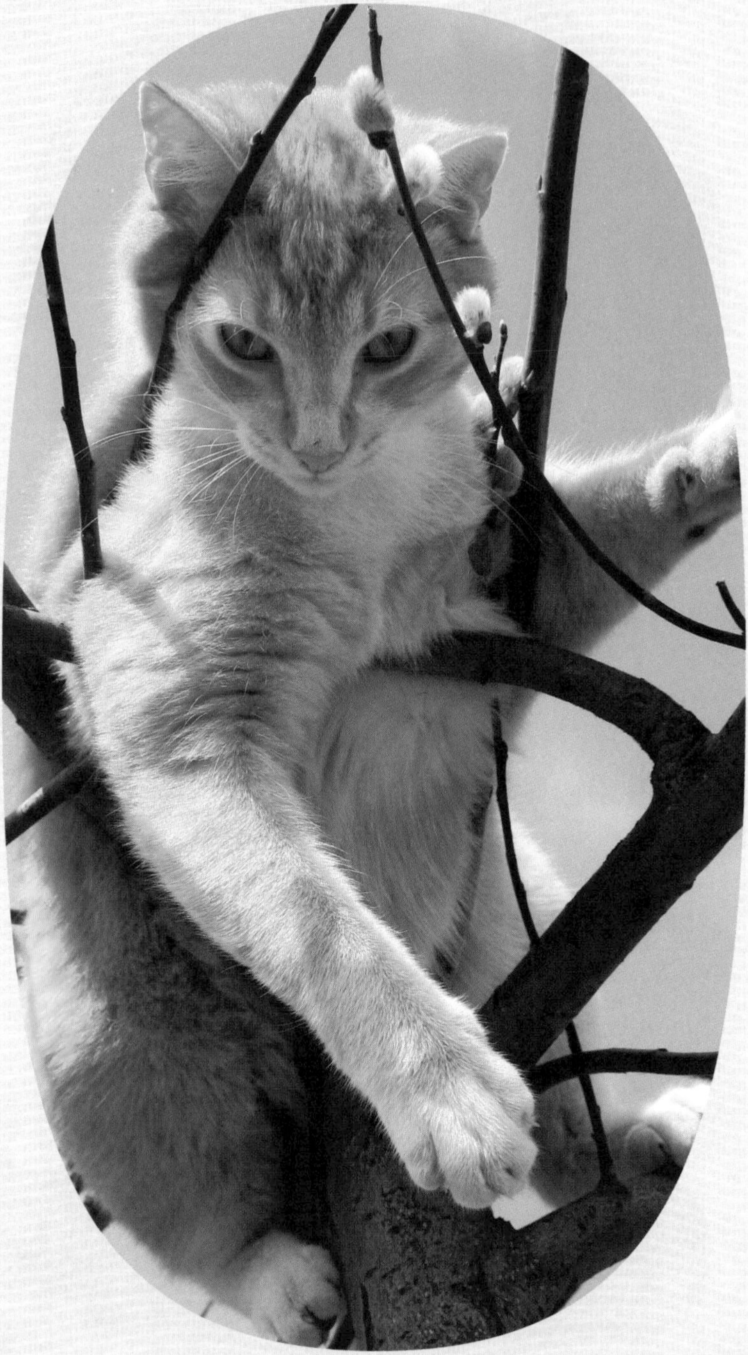

VERSE 62

The gods even envy him
whose senses, like horses
well broken in by the driver,
have been subdued, who is
free from pride, and free
from appetites.

Pride and desire are stressful and destructive emotions.
Control them, and you'll find peace in your life.

VERSE 63

If a man would hasten towards the good, he should keep his thought away from evil; if a man does what is good slothfully, his mind delights in evil.

Doing good things quickly and often keeps your mind and heart away from bad ideas.

VERSE 64

Let no man think lightly of good, saying in his heart, It will not come nigh unto me. Even by the falling of water-drops a water-pot is filled; the wise man becomes full of good, even if he gather it little by little.

Fretting about imperfections won't solve them. If you gather good deeds day by day, you'll have benefited the world many times over the course of your life.

VERSE 65

Let a man avoid evil deeds, as a merchant,
if he has few companions and carries much
wealth, avoids a dangerous road; as a man
who loves life avoids poison.

Your life and time is precious, spend it with
people who value life as much as you do.

VERSE 66

If a man offend a harmless, pure, and innocent person, the evil falls back upon that fool, like light dust thrown up against the wind.

There are many times in life when we accidentally hurt innocent people. Be conscientious with your actions, even when they don't have an obvious effect on others.

VERSE 67

Not nakedness, not platted hair, not dirt, not fasting, or lying on the earth, not rubbing with dust, not sitting motionless, can purify a mortal who has not overcome desires.

A million apologies or prayers won't fix someone who refuses to truly change. Only actions can lead people out of their bad habits.

VERSE 68

Well-makers lead the water (wherever they like); fletchers bend the arrow; carpenters bend a log of wood; good people fashion themselves.

Think of yourself as a sculpture to be continually formed and made into something more beautiful. It takes work to become a better person.

VERSE 69

The brilliant chariots of kings are destroyed, the body also approaches destruction, but the virtue of good people never approaches destruction,— thus do the good say to the good.

Material things, even great statues and monuments, will all crumble eventually. But a virtuous life, and its effects on loved ones, will last into eternity.

VERSE 70

He whose wickedness is very great brings himself down to that state where his enemy wishes him to be, as a creeper does with the tree which it surrounds.

If someone wishes you ill, his goal is to bring you down a notch, so you'll stray from your path.

VERSE 71

Bad deeds, and deeds hurtful to ourselves, are easy to do; what is beneficial and good, that is very difficult to do.

Being good isn't easy to do, but the payoff is greater. Evil, on the other hand, is easy and attractive.

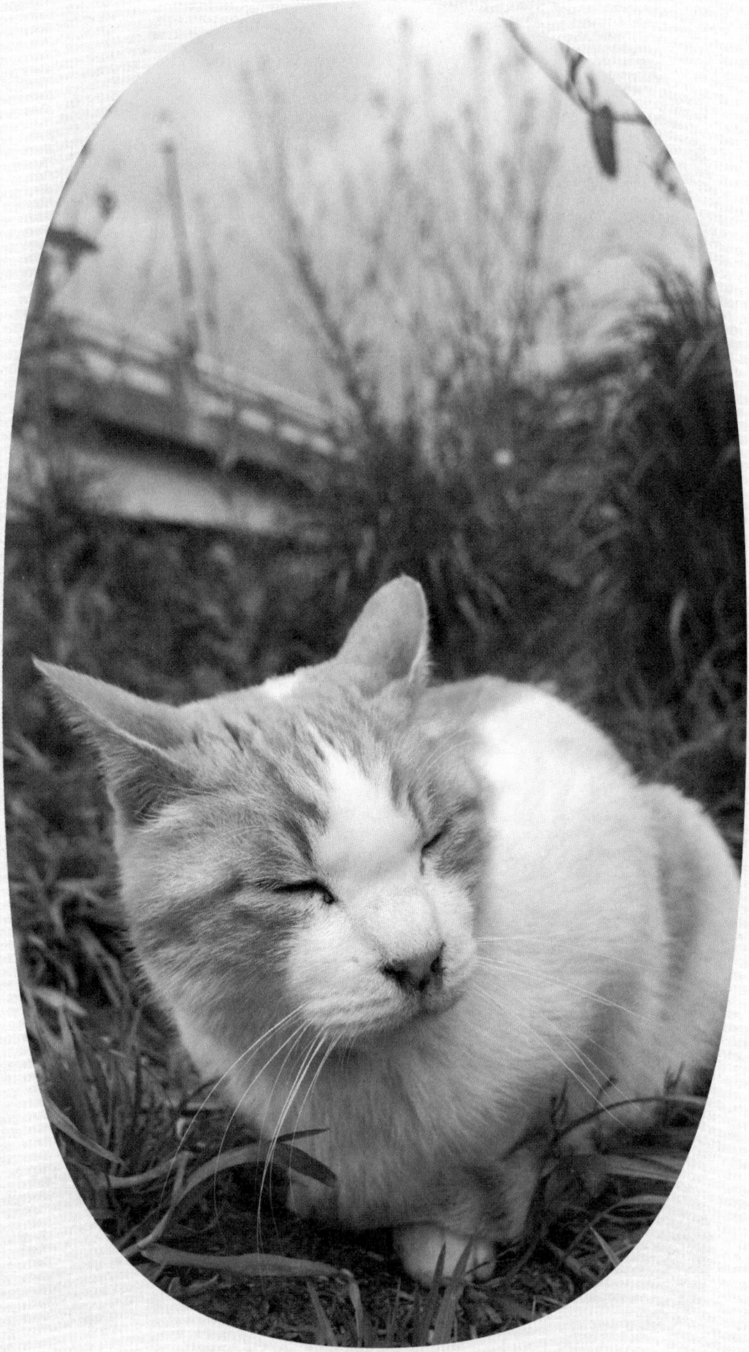

VERSE 72

Follow the law of virtue; do not follow that of sin. The virtuous rests in bliss in this world and in the next.

Virtue may be difficult to achieve, but it provides peace of mind and happiness in both life and death.

VERSE 73

What ought to be done is neglected, what ought not to be done is done; the desires of unruly, thoughtless people are always increasing.

Evil increases only if you allow it to. If your purpose is clear, your actions will follow.

VERSE 74

Good people shine from afar, like the snowy mountains; bad people are not seen, like arrows shot by night.

While goodness may not always bring riches or power, it will always be part of how people value and remember you.

VERSE 75

An evil deed is better left undone, for a man repents of it afterwards; a good deed is better done, for having done it, one does not repent.

If you're going to regret something after you do it, it's probably a bad idea. A good deed never brings regret.

VERSE 76

Pleasant is virtue lasting to old age, pleasant is a faith firmly rooted; pleasant is attainment of intelligence, pleasant is avoiding of sins.

Your soul will feel fulfilled if you have a virtuous life, spiritual faith, and great knowledge to fall back on in your old age.

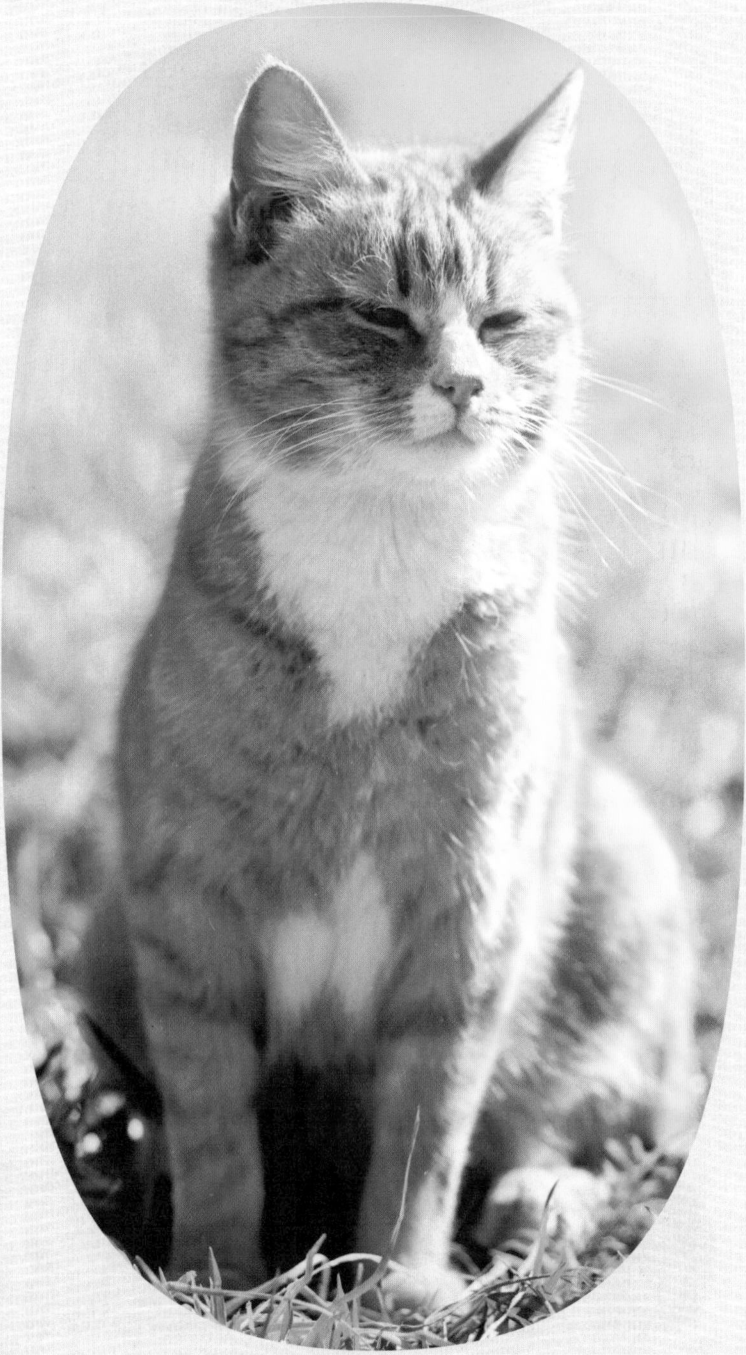

VERSE 77

Him I call indeed enlightened who does not cling to pleasures, like water on a lotus leaf, like a mustard seed on the point of a needle.

The enlightened soul gives up on the petty desires of daily life and always looks at the big picture.

TRUTH

VERSE 78

They who imagine truth in
untruth, and see untruth in
truth, never arrive at truth,
but follow vain desires.

Intuition can be flawed. Ideas should be contemplated
thoroughly to determine if they are wise.

VERSE 79

If a traveller does not meet with one who is his better, or his equal, let him firmly keep to his solitary journey; there is no companionship with a fool.

Solitude may be unpopular, but it is better to be good alone than do evil with many.

VERSE 80

The fool who knows his foolishness, is wise at least so far. But a fool who thinks himself wise, he is called a fool indeed.

Your wisdom is always growing. Keep your mind open to new ideas as life presents new challenges.

VERSE 81

If a fool be associated with a wise man even all his life, he will perceive the truth as little as a spoon perceives the taste of soup.

There are plenty of caring, wise people in your life worth listening to. Be receptive to their ideas in times of trouble.

VERSE 82

As a solid rock is not shaken by the wind, wise people falter not amidst blame and praise.

Be true to your judgment if it is made wisely, though it will be faced with criticism.

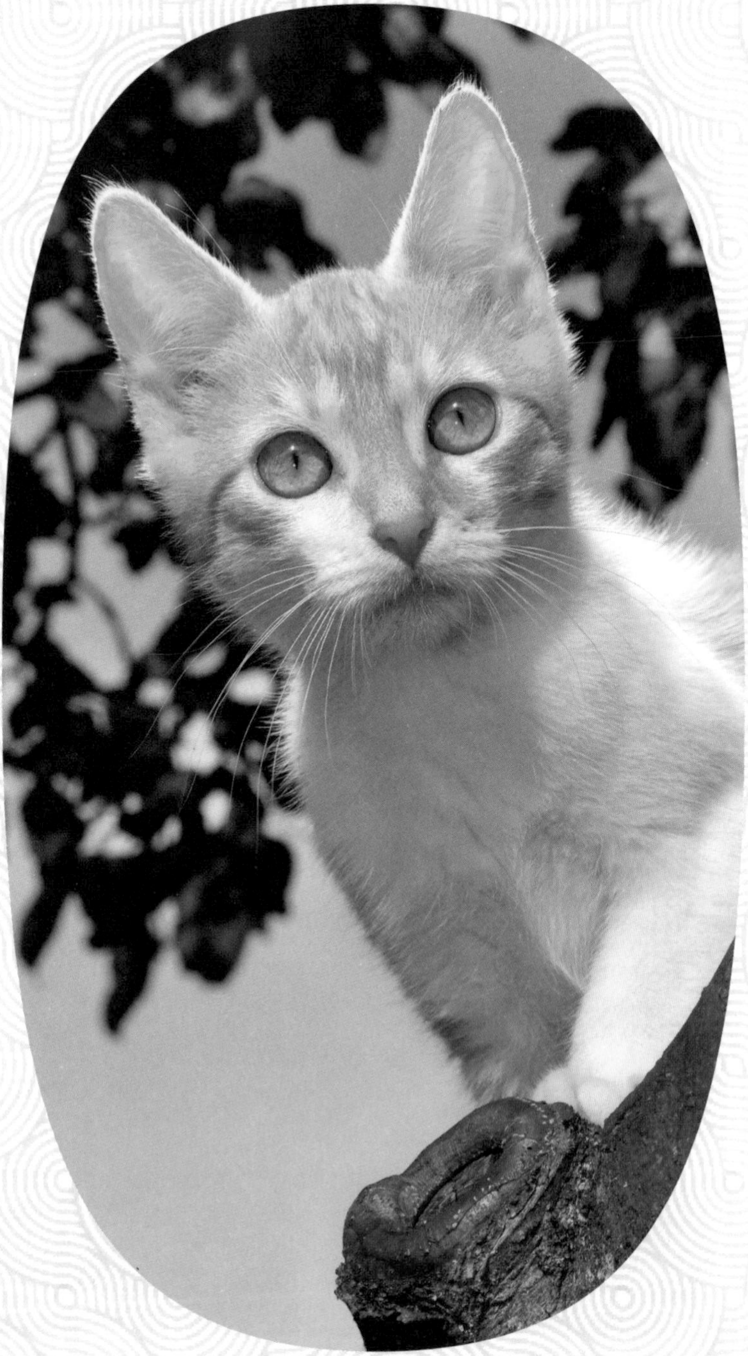

VERSE 83

Wise people, after they have
listened to the laws, become
serene, like a deep, smooth,
and still lake.

The truth will free your mind. Even hard truths will
provide a sense of clarity in chaotic doubt.

VERSE 84

Even though a speech be a thousand
words, but made up of senseless words,
one word of sense is better, which if a
man hears, he becomes quiet.

Words can be used in many ways that are untruthful.
A wise person keeps his words limited and honest,
and offers them when needed.

VERSE 85

And he who lives a hundred years, ignorant and unrestrained, a life of one day is better if a man is wise and reflecting.

A reflecting mind is open to growth and change throughout a life. To live every day without reflection is to live the same day over and over, without growth.

VERSE 86

All men tremble at punishment, all men love life; remember that thou art like unto them, and do not kill, nor cause slaughter.

A stranger is only a stranger in name, he wants the same things you do. Always treat him as you would yourself.

VERSE 87

Is there in this world any man so restrained by humility that he does not mind reproof, as a well-trained horse the whip?

Humility allows for clarity in observing one's own flaws. Criticism received without pride allows for true change to occur.

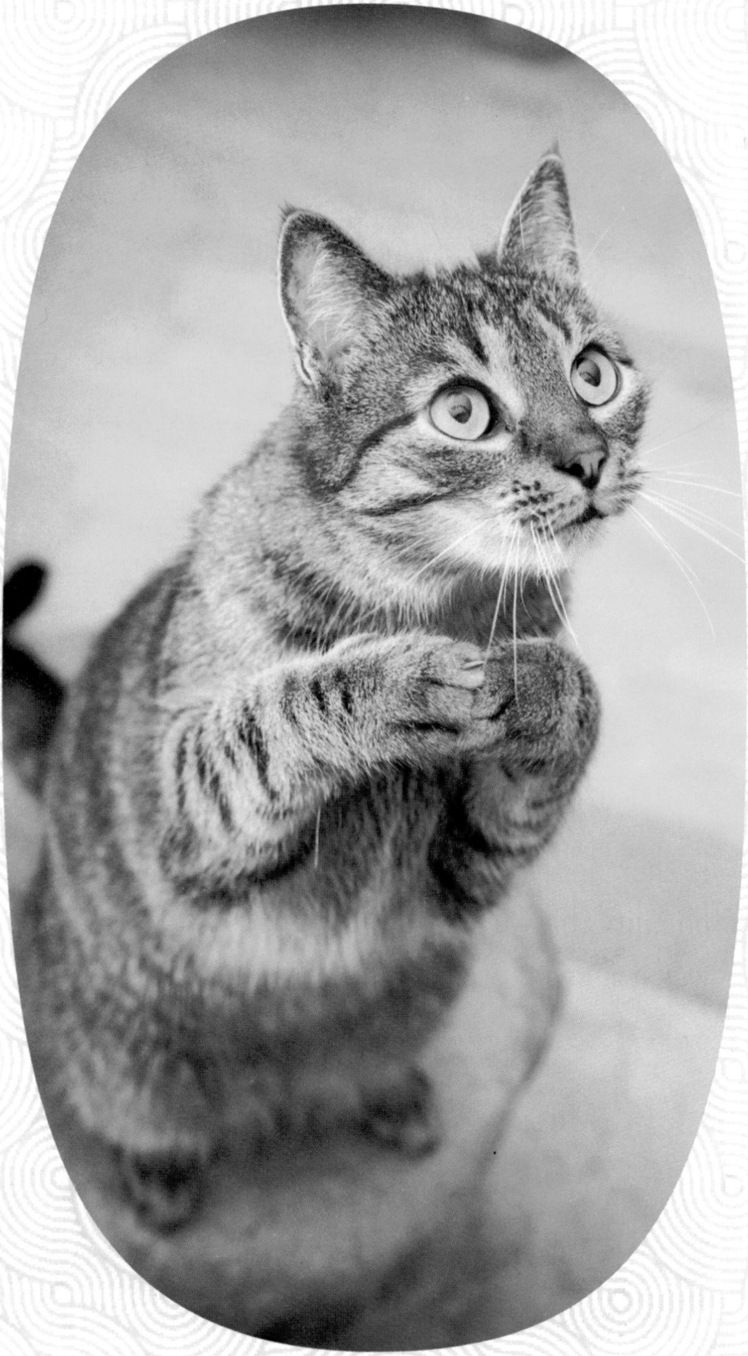

VERSE 88

A man who has learnt little, grows old like an ox; his flesh grows, but his knowledge does not grow.

Age does not always bring wisdom. Without contemplation and curiosity, a person will merely become a plain, weathered rock.

VERSE 89

Men who have not observed proper discipline,
and have not gained treasure in their youth,
perish like old herons in a lake without fish.

Youth can be a time of fun, but it is also filled with
enormous potential. If youth is spent pursuing truth in
oneself and the world, it will pay off in later years.

VERSE 90

Let no one forget his own duty for the sake of another's, however great; let a man, after he has discerned his own duty, be always attentive to his duty.

A person's responsibility belongs to him or her alone. Reflect on actions that feel both virtuous and fulfilling, and follow that path to your purpose.

VERSE 91

Do not follow the evil law! Do not live on in thoughtlessness! Do not follow false doctrine! Be not a friend of the world.

The ways of the world often lead us astray. Seek to be a friend to humanity and you will remain on a virtuous road.

VERSE 92

Come, look at this glittering world, like unto a royal chariot; the foolish are immersed in it, but the wise do not touch it.

Though the world's delights may glitter and seem attractive, there is often a lie waiting under the façade. The meaningful things in life are difficult to obtain.

VERSE 93

He who formerly was reckless
and afterwards became sober,
brightens up this world, like the
moon when freed from clouds.

It is never too late to become wise and caring. To become a
beacon of truth in the darkness is a worthy calling for every
person, however flawed.

VERSE 94

Not to commit any sin, to do good, and to purify one's mind, that is the teaching of (all) the Awakened.

Good things are often hard to do, but it's often very simple to perceive what is good. All that stands in the way is the will to do good.

VERSE 95

Therefore, one ought to follow the wise, the intelligent, the learned, the much enduring, the dutiful, the elect; one ought to follow a good and wise man, as the moon follows the path of the stars.

It is tempting to only be guided by charming people, but there is little to be learned from them. The wisest friends to have are those who will stick around when the party is done.

VERSE 96

He who possesses virtue and intelligence, who is just, speaks the truth, and does what is his own business, him the world will hold dear.

Though fashionable people will be forgotten, the truthful and earnest carry on in the good they have brought to the world.

VERSE 97

Let a man leave anger, let him forsake pride, let him overcome all bondage! No sufferings befall the man who is not attached to name and form, and who calls nothing his own.

Chains come in different forms, and attachment is one of them. Remain attached to truth, rather than the fleeting elements of life: money, people and power.

VERSE 98

Let a man overcome anger by love,
let him overcome evil by good;
let him overcome the greedy by
liberality, the liar by truth!

Every evil thing can be overcome with its opposite.
Strive to always be in opposition to evil with humility,
love, and honesty.

VERSE 99

Speak the truth, do not yield to anger; give,
if thou art asked for little; by these three
steps thou wilt go near the gods.

Truthfulness, patience, and generosity are the qualities
that create lasting love and happiness in life.

VERSE 100

A man is not learned because he talks much; he who is patient, free from hatred and fear, he is called learned.

Intelligence is not defined by being the loudest voice in the room. Often it is quiet people who are the wisest, because they listen.

VERSE 101

If anything is to be done, let a man do it, let him attack it vigorously! A careless pilgrim only scatters the dust of his passions more widely.

Live life to the fullest by pursuing passions with intent and discipline, rather than succumbing to self-doubt.

VERSE 102

They who fear when they ought not to fear, and fear not when they ought to fear, such men, embracing false doctrines, enter the evil path.

Fear can snuff out all rational thought and compassion. Approach challenges, however hard, with understanding and courage.

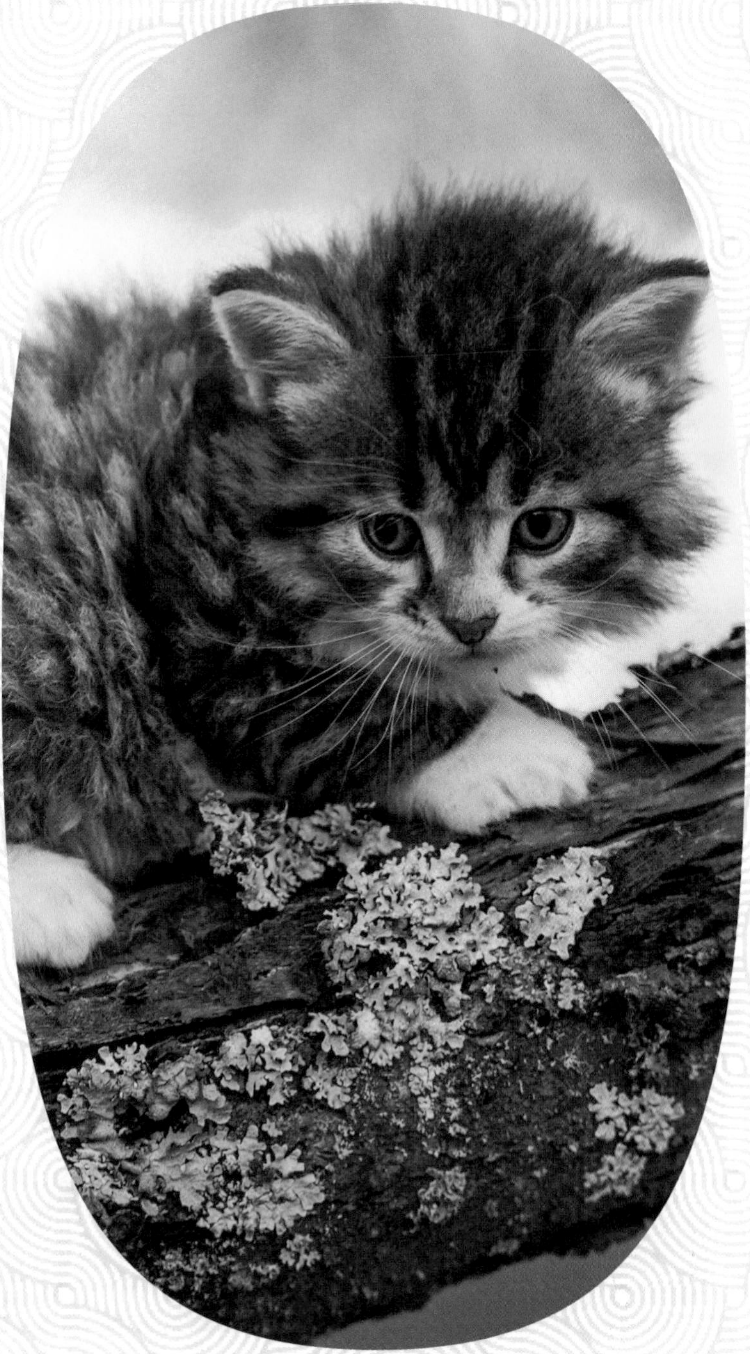

VERSE 103

It is better to live alone, there is no companionship with a fool; let a man walk alone, let him commit no sin, with few wishes, like an elephant in the forest.

A good companion can increase your wisdom many times over, but self-reliance is important when there is no virtuous friend to be found.

VERSE 104

Without knowledge there is no meditation, without meditation there is no knowledge: he who has knowledge and meditation is near unto Nirvana.

Intelligent thoughts, for most, do not appear out of thin air. Meditation allows the mind to weigh all sides fairly.

VERSE 105

Him I call indeed enlightened who finds no fault with other beings, whether feeble or strong, and does not kill nor cause slaughter.

Value others' good qualities above all. Criticism can be a good way to work out flaws, but looking for flaws where there are none is simply a waste.

VERSE 106

Him I call indeed enlightened who is tolerant
with the intolerant, mild with fault-finders,
and free from passion among the passionate.

It is easy to dismiss those who embrace intolerance.
Instead, try to understand the very human conditions
that breed anger and hate.

VERSE 107

Him I call indeed enlightened who utters true speech, instructive and free from harshness, so that he offend no one.

Everyone has the ability to teach rather than scold.
It is simply a matter of being gentle and true when speaking.

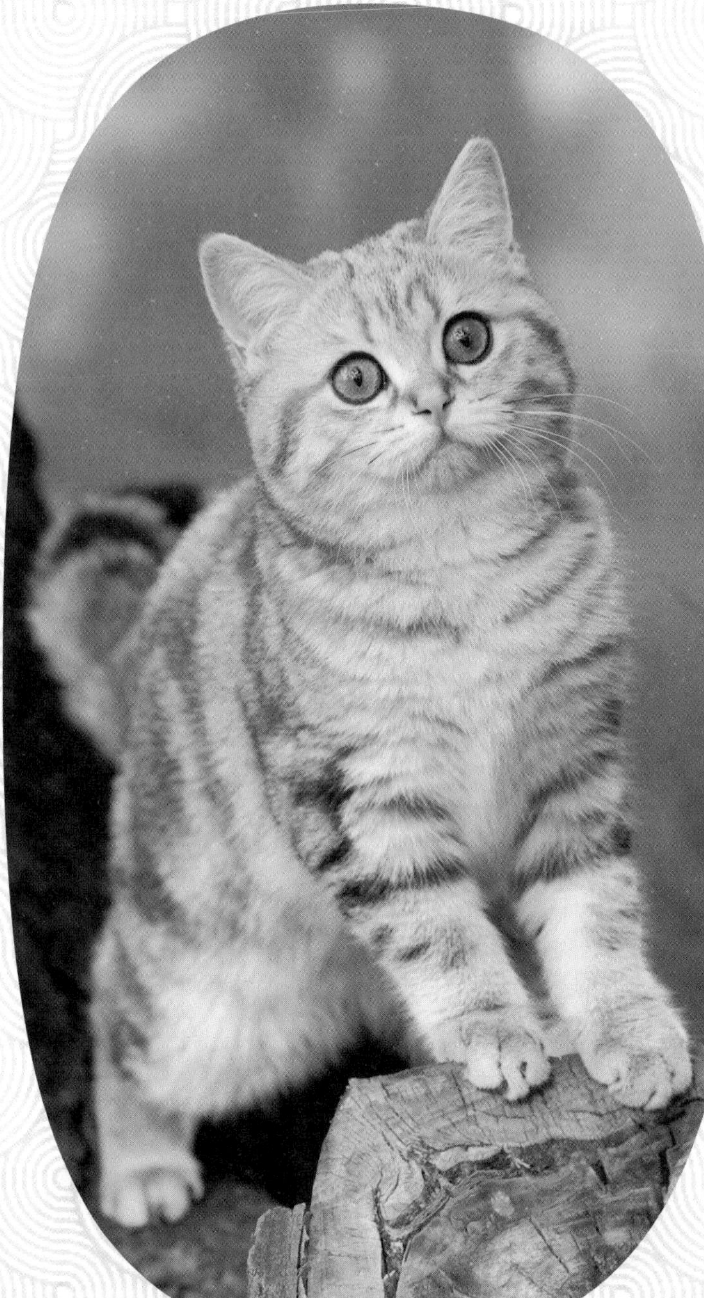

VERSE 108

Him I call indeed
enlightened who in this
world is above good and evil,
above the bondage of both,
free from grief from sin, and
from impurity.

Enlightenment comes from within. Though it is useful to listen
to others, true goodness will only come with action.

ETERNITY

VERSE 109

The virtuous man is happy in this world,
and he is happy in the next; he is happy
in both. He is happy when he thinks of
the good he has done; he is still more
happy when going on the good path.

A good person who acts kindly will always find happiness.
It is only when worldly concerns seep in that unhappiness
brews in the mind.

VERSE 110

The world does not know that we must all come to an end here;—but those who know it, their quarrels cease at once.

Life is too short to fill with grudges and arguments. While dwelling on death is distracting, it is good to remember that time is precious.

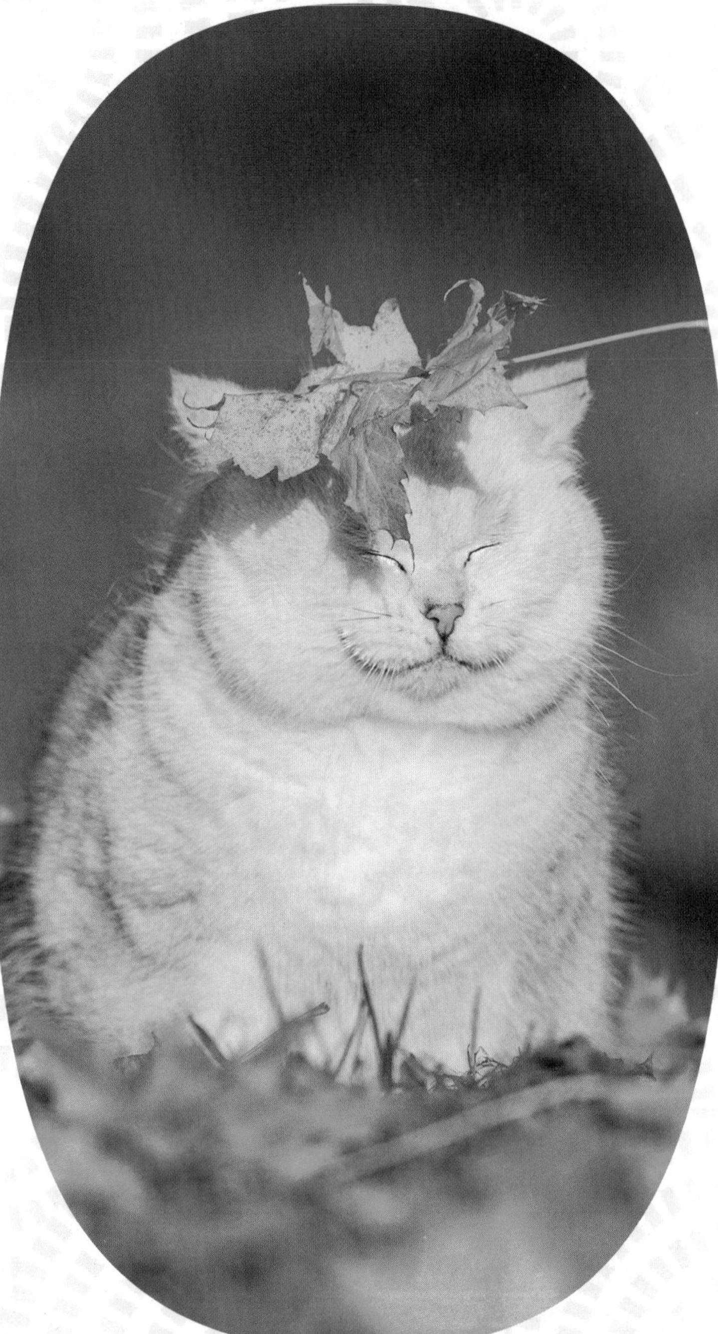

VERSE 111

The evil-doer mourns in this world, and he mourns in the next; he mourns in both. He mourns and suffers when he sees the evil of his own work.

Those who delight from evil are not truly happy and their acts will not live on after they have passed.

VERSE 112

Earnestness is the path of immortality (Nirvana), thoughtlessness the path of death. Those who are in earnest do not die, those who are thoughtless are as if dead already.

Those who are earnest and giving in life will live on in the memories of everyone they touched.

VERSE 113

He who knows that this body is like froth, and has learnt that it is as unsubstantial as a mirage, will break the flower-pointed arrow of Mara, and never see the king of death.

The world's demands are temporary, eternity is found in a life full of love for others.

VERSE 114

There is no suffering for him who has finished his journey, and abandoned grief, who has freed himself on all sides, and thrown off all fetters.

Life's suffering is only temporary. Those who can weather it with patience and kindness will reach Nirvana.

VERSE 115

This world is dark, few only can see here; a few only go to heaven, like birds escaped from the net.

Be among the people who see with clarity in the chaos of the world. When your life has passed, you will know that you left the world a little brighter.

VERSE 116

All created things perish.
He who knows and sees this
becomes passive in pain; this
is the way to purity.

All things, however good or bad, will come to an end.
When one understands that suffering is temporary, it is
easier to endure the pain.

VERSE 117

Death comes and carries off that man, praised for his children and flocks, his mind distracted, as a flood carries off a sleeping village.

Life will pass by those who are caught up in petty details. Be aware always of the short time that is given to you on this earth.

VERSE 118

A creature's pleasures are extravagant and luxurious; sunk in lust and looking for pleasure, men undergo (again and again) birth and decay.

One can only find peace of mind when he has abandoned constant desire. Lack of satisfaction is not appeased with time, but with contemplation of what really matters.

VERSE 119

Give up what is before, give up what is
behind, give up what is in the middle, when
thou goest to the other shore of existence;
if thy mind is altogether free, thou wilt
not again enter into birth and decay.

Live life so that when your time comes to depart, you
will have no regrets to disturb your peace.

VERSE 120

Let him live in charity, let him be perfect in his duties; then in the fullness of delight he will make an end of suffering.

Delight in making the world a better place and you will find peace in death. If you have lived by example, others will carry your torch.

CREDITS